LINDSEY HORAN

BY LEIGH LEWIS

Inspire is published by
Amicus Learning, an imprint of Amicus
P.O. Box 227
Mankato, MN 56002
www.amicuspublishing.us

Editor: Ana Brauer
Series Designer: Kathleen Petelinsek
Book Designer and Photo Researcher: Emily Dietz

Library of Congress Cataloging-in-Publication Data
Names: Lewis, Leigh, author.
Title: Lindsey Horan / By Leigh Lewis.
Description: Mankato, MN : Amicus Learning, [2026] | Series: Inspire | Includes bibliographical
    references and index. | Audience: Ages 5–9 | Audience: Grades 2–3 | Summary: "Learn about
    soccer star Lindsey Horan and her accomplishments in an engaging profile packed with photos and
    fact-filled text suitable for young readers. Includes table of contents, glossary, further resources, and
    index"— Provided by publisher.
Identifiers: LCCN 2024044105 (print) | LCCN 2024044106 (ebook) | ISBN 9798892005203 (library binding) |
    ISBN 9798892005746 (paperback) | ISBN 9798892006286 (ebook)
Subjects: LCSH: Horan, Lindsey,—Juvenile literature. | Soccer midfielders—United States—
    Biography—Juvenile literature. | Soccer midfielders—France—Biography—Juvenile
    literature. | Women soccer players—United States—Biography—Juvenile literature. |
    Women soccer players—France—Biography—Juvenile literature. | Soccer—United
    States—Juvenile literature. | Soccer—France—Juvenile literature. | Olympique
    Lyonnais Féminin (Soccer team)—Juvenile literature.
Classification: LCC GV942.7.H653 L48 2026 (print) | LCC GV942.7.H653 (ebook) |
    DDC 796.334092 [B]—dc23/eng/20241210
LC record available at https://lccn.loc.gov/2024044105
LC ebook record available at https://lccn.loc.gov/2024044106

Photo Credits: Alamy Stock Photo/Brenton Tse/ZUMA Press Wire, cover; Associated
Press/Andrew Dieb, 12; Getty Images/AAron Ontiveroz, 7, Andy Lyons/USSF,
20–21, ANP, 16, Hannah Peters - FIFA, 4, Icon Sportswire, 14, John Todd/ISI,
18, Molly Darlington - AMA, 11, NurPhoto, 17, Xavier Laine, 8; Shutterstock/
irin-k, 19, Julia Babii, 10, Mr.Music, 9, QubixStudio, 10

Printed in India

Table of Contents

Lindsey Horan is one of the best female soccer players in the world.

Soccer Star

Lindsey Horan runs. She protects the goal. She passes. She scores! As a **midfielder**, she does it all. Lindsey Horan is an American soccer star. She is captain of the United States Women's National Team (USWNT).

Early Days

Horan's mom was her coach until she was 11. In 2005, Horan joined a **club team** called Colorado Rush. She played with them until 2012. She planned to play soccer at the University of North Carolina.

Young Horan
dreamed of being
a great soccer player
and made it come true.

Horan played with Paris
Saint-Germain from
2012 until 2016.

Going Pro

Instead of college, Horan went pro at 17. In 2012, she moved to France after high school. Her team was called Paris Saint-Germain. It wasn't easy because she was alone. She didn't speak French, but she learned quickly.

A Winning Team

In 2013, Horan was asked to represent the US in the USWNT. In 2019, Horan helped them win the World Cup. It is the most important tournament in soccer. Players play for their own countries.

DID YOU KNOW?
Soccer players sometimes play for a club team and their country's team in the same year. Horan has played for French and American club teams, and for the USWNT.

Horan cheers with her
team after winning the
2019 FIFA Women's
World Cup.

11

Horan started playing as a midfielder for the USWNT in 2016.

Switching Positions

Horan played **forward** for three years. Her main job was to score goals. She scored a lot of them! In 2016, her coach switched her to midfield. She became a leader on the field. She helps control the game.

Horan fights for control of the ball during the NWSL championship game in 2017.

She Shoots, She Scores!

Horan returned to the US in 2016. She played for the Portland Thorns. In 2017, Horan scored the winning goal in the National Women's Soccer League (NWSL) championship match. In 2018, she was named the Most Valuable Player (MVP).

Back to France

In 2022, Horan returned to France to play for Lyon. The Portland Thorns lent her to the French team. Lyon represented France in the **UEFA** Women's Champions League. They won! In 2023, Horan decided to play for Lyon permanently.

RECORD HOLDER
Lyon has won the Women's Champions League eight times. That is the most wins of any club ever.

In 2023, Horan
signed a three
year contract
with Lyon.

Horan often uses her head to score goals.

18

Three-Time Olympian

Horan and the USWNT played in the 2016 Rio Olympics. They also played in the 2020 Tokyo games. Her team won a bronze medal there. In 2024, Horan was captain of the USWNT for the Paris Olympics. Horan led her team to a gold medal!

HAT TRICK
Horan scored her first hat trick in a game that helped the US get into the 2020 Tokyo Olympics.

Horan loves
meeting her fans.
Speaking Up

In France, Horan was bullied for her weight.
Even though she played well, her coaches told
her to be thinner. It hurt Horan. She spoke up.
She says not to listen to that kind of talk.
She inspires kids to follow their dreams.

LINDSEY MICHELLE HORAN

Nicknames: The Great Horan

Birthday: May 26, 1994

Hometown: Golden, Colorado

Position: Midfielder

Current Teams: Lyon (Olympique Lyonnais, in France) and USWNT

ACCOMPLISHMENTS

US Soccer Young Female Player of the Year: 2013

Olympic Medals: Bronze in 2020, Gold in 2024

NWSL Championship MVP: 2017

NWSL MVP: 2018

US Soccer Female Player of the Year: 2021

US Women's National Team Captain: 2023–2024

At least one goal per year for USWNT since 2015.

GLOSSARY

club team A private team that is not part of a school.

forward The players closest to the other team's goal whose job it is to score goals.

hat trick When a player scores three goals in one game.

midfielder A soccer player who plays between the forwards and the defense.

UEFA The Union of European Football Association is the group that oversees soccer in Europe.

READ MORE

Calkhoven, Laurie. **Squad Goals: The Unstoppable Women of the US Women's National Soccer Team.** New York, NY: Simon Spotlight, 2023.

Schwartz, Heather E. **US Women's National Soccer Team: Winning On and Off the Field.** Minneapolis, MN: Lerner Publications, 2024.

ON THE WEB

Team USA Lindsey Horan
https://www.teamusa.com/profiles/
lindsey-horan-817502

US Soccer Lindsey Horan
https://www.ussoccer.com/
players/h/lindsey-horan

INDEX

About the Author

Leigh Lewis is a children's author who loves her three kids, traveling, pickleball, and telling stories. She has lived in the US, Russia, Japan, England, Greece, and Turkey. Check out her books at leighlewisbooks.com.